Water
for Life

Terry Jennings
Photographs by Jenny Matthews
Illustrations by Peter Bull Art Studio

A & C Black · London

Contents

Cover photographs
Front – Making a water filter (see page 12)
Back – Dam at Llyn Clywedog, near Llanidloes, Powys (see page 11)

Title page photograph – Panoramic view of Thomson's Falls, Nyahururu, Kenya

Acknowledgements
Photographs by Jenny Matthews except for: p.9, p.14/15 (bottom), p.16, p.17 (bottom), p.19 (top), p.24 (middle), p.25 (middle) Terry Jennings; p.11 (top), p.13 (bottom), p.22, p.24 (bottom), p.25 (top), p.26 (top and bottom) Mark Edwards/Still Pictures; title page Gryniewicz, p.13 (top) Janulewicz, p.17 (top) Morgan, p.18 (all) Morgan/Platt, p.23 (top) Corbett, p.24 (top) Cooper, p.25 (bottom) Meech, Ecoscene; p.15 (top and middle) Liba Taylor; p.19 (bottom) Peter Johnson/NHPA; p.23 (middle) Douglas Dickins.

The author and publisher would like to thank the following people for their invaluable help during the preparation of this book: the staff and pupils of Rushmore Junior School, especially Chris Taylor.

A CIP record for this book is available from the British Library.

ISBN 0-7136-3542-8

First published 1992 A & C Black (Publishers) Ltd
35 Bedford Row, London WC1R 4JH

Typeset by Rowland Phototypesetting Ltd,
Bury St Edmunds, Suffolk
Printed in Italy by Imago

What do we use water for?

Water is one of the most important substances on Earth. Without it there would be no living things. About 70% of your body weight is water while some simple plants and animals are 99% water!

Water makes up a large proportion of what we eat and drink. Having water to drink, however, is far more important than having food. People have lived for a month or more without food, but we could only last for three or four days without water.

In America, each person uses an average of 600 litres of water a day. In some countries without piped water, people make do with as little as 10 litres a day.

Nearly three quarters of the Earth's surface is covered with water. But most of it is salty seawater or ice and is therefore unsuitable for human use.

On average we each use about 150 litres of water a day – that's 15 bucketfuls! Some of the things we use water for are:–

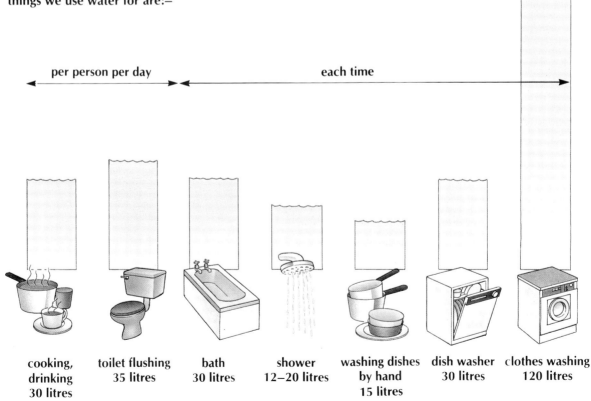

| per person per day | each time |

cooking, drinking 30 litres
toilet flushing 35 litres
bath 30 litres
shower 12–20 litres
washing dishes by hand 15 litres
dish washer 30 litres
clothes washing 120 litres

Keep a drinks diary

Estimate how much water you drink every day. Keep a drinks diary. You could pour each drink into a measuring jug and record its volume. Don't forget that drinks like milk, tea, coffee and orange squash are almost all water.

How much water is there in your food?

1 Cut a fresh potato into slices and weigh all the pieces.

2 Put them in a warm place until they are completely dry.

3 Weigh them again. How much weight have the pieces of potato lost?

That weight is the amount of water the potato contained. Try this experiment with other foods.

5

The water cycle

The water on Earth moves from the seas to the air, back to the ground again as rain, along rivers and through plants and eventually back to the sea again. This movement of water, known as the water cycle, enables us to use the water again and again.

The water cycle

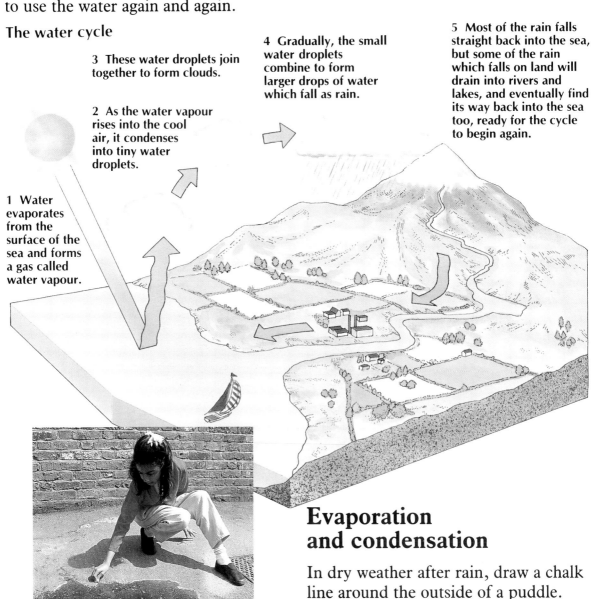

1 Water evaporates from the surface of the sea and forms a gas called water vapour.

2 As the water vapour rises into the cool air, it condenses into tiny water droplets.

3 These water droplets join together to form clouds.

4 Gradually, the small water droplets combine to form larger drops of water which fall as rain.

5 Most of the rain falls straight back into the sea, but some of the rain which falls on land will drain into rivers and lakes, and eventually find its way back into the sea too, ready for the cycle to begin again.

Evaporation and condensation

In dry weather after rain, draw a chalk line around the outside of a puddle. During the rest of the day, watch to see how much water evaporates from the puddle.

Take a small jar, such as a paste jar, and a saucer. Fill them both with the same amount of water and stand them on a sunny windowsill. From which container does all the water evaporate first? Why is this?

Cooling steam

Steam is made up of tiny water droplets which have formed as water vapour has cooled. You can see how the water droplets turn into drops of water if you cool steam.

1 Ask an adult to boil a kettle of water. Wearing gloves, carefully hold a large metal spoon or ladle in the steam.

2 In a saucer, catch the drops of water that fall from the ladle. When water vapour or steam turns back into liquid water it is said to condense.

Make a rain gauge

Make a rain gauge from a washing-up liquid bottle like this. Ask an adult to help you to cut the bottle. Stand the rain gauge out in the open. Carefully pour each day's rain into a small bottle. Do this for a week. On which day did most rain fall?

The Water Supply

We need clean water for drinking, cooking and washing. In one year, you probably use about 55 000 litres of water – enough to fill a large tanker lorry. This water has to be clean and safe to use.

Many people in the world still get their water from a stream or well. However, in places which are densely populated, such as towns and cities, streams and wells cannot provide enough water to cope with the demand. Water is therefore taken from lakes, rivers or reservoirs. A reservoir is a large artificial lake made by building a dam across a river.

How water is cleaned

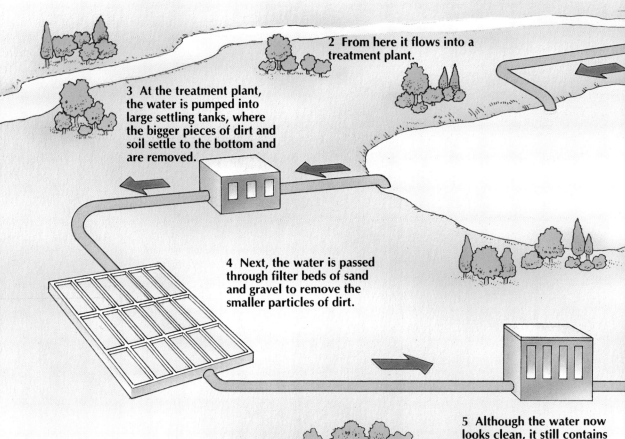

1 Water is pumped from the base of a dam to a service reservoir.

2 From here it flows into a treatment plant.

3 At the treatment plant, the water is pumped into large settling tanks, where the bigger pieces of dirt and soil settle to the bottom and are removed.

4 Next, the water is passed through filter beds of sand and gravel to remove the smaller particles of dirt.

5 Although the water now looks clean, it still contains harmful germs which are too small to be filtered out. Chlorine gas is added to the water to destroy these bacteria.

▶ Whenever possible, reservoirs are built high up in hills or mountains where they can be fed by clean streams.

Many people do not like dams and reservoirs. Why do you think this is? What do they do to the scenery? What effect do they have on farmland and on wildlife?

6 Now the water is clean and fit to drink, and is pumped along large underground pipes called water mains. Water not needed immediately is pumped into storage towers or service reservoirs.

Make a water filter

1 With the help of an adult, carefully cut the bottom off a clean plastic lemonade bottle.

2 Hold the bottle upside down and put a layer of cotton wool in what is now the bottom. On top of this put a thick layer of clean washed sand, a thick layer of clean washed gravel and finally a circle of paper. Stand your filter over a clean jar.

3 Mix up some soil and water to make muddy water. Carefully pour it into the filter.

4 Does the filtered water look clean? It still isn't fit to drink. Why is this?

Try your filter with salt water and water with ink in it. Does your filter remove the salt and ink?

In countries such as Niger, where water is in short supply, children may spend several hours of every day fetching water to take back to their homes.

We are used to turning on the tap and getting clean, pure water. But at least two-thirds of the people in the world still fetch their water from pumps, wells or water-holes in the ground. In many places, people have to spend hours every day fetching and carrying water. Often the water they get is unclean and contains harmful germs. Up to 22 million children are believed to die each year from either lack of water or from drinking dirty water.

How much water does a dripping tap waste?

Measure how much water drips from a dripping tap in an hour. How much water would be lost in a day? In a week? In a year?

What you can do

Don't use more water than you need. This saves water and results in less sewage. It also means fewer reservoirs are needed.

✳ Collect your own rain water. Use it to clean cars and to water plants.

✳ Save water in dry weather by using washing-up water on your garden.

✳ Ask your parents to put a brick in the toilet cistern so that it will not use so much water each time it is flushed.

✳ Save water by taking a shower instead of a bath.

11

Putting water to work

Industry uses vast quantities of water. As countries become more industrialised, the amount of water they use increases considerably. Most of this water comes from lakes and rivers.

Paper mills are often built beside lakes or rivers because paper-making uses such a large amount of water. Paper is made from a pulp of water and wood; just to make a single comic takes 9 litres of water.

It takes:-

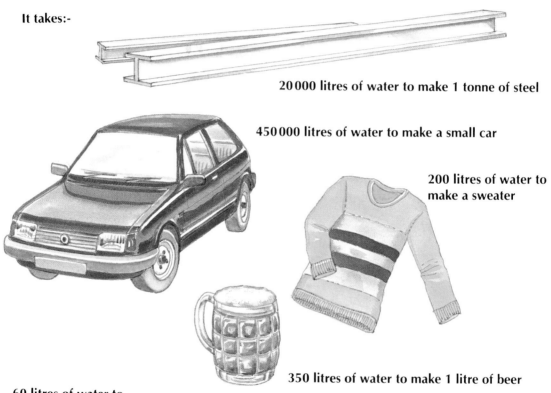

20 000 litres of water to make 1 tonne of steel

450 000 litres of water to make a small car

200 litres of water to make a sweater

350 litres of water to make 1 litre of beer

60 litres of water to make a pair of shoes

Water is also used for cooling industrial processes. A large power station, for example, uses steam to drive its generators and needs 200 000 litres of water every hour to cool the steam and turn it back into water. The resulting hot water is very often pumped into a nearby sea, river or lake affecting the plant and animal life. Some plants grow very quickly in the warm conditions and choke the water, while some fish are unable to breed.

This coal-fired power station needs cooling towers to cool the steam which drives its generators. What effect do you think the building of these power stations could have on the scenery and wildlife of an area?

▼ Do you think hydroelectric power stations, like this one in Tanzania, and tidal power stations are better than those which use coal, gas, oil or nuclear energy? Why?

In a few areas the waste water from power stations is used to heat nearby houses and factories.

Some 2000 years ago, the Romans first used the power of fast-flowing rivers to turn stones which ground corn into flour. Nowadays, hydroelectric power stations use the power of falling water to drive generators which make electricity.

Water for growing plants

Without water, most plants will quickly die. Many plants contain a high percentage of water. For example, a melon is 99% water, a pineapple 87% and a tomato 95%.

Where does the water go to in a plant?

Stand a flower such as a carnation or a daisy in coloured water. You can colour the water with ink or a food colouring. Can you see where the water goes? How long does it take to travel up into the flower's petals?

Trees and other plants use up vast amounts of water. In one day, a large oak tree can take in 20000 litres of water. That's the equivalent of 600 bathfuls. Most of this water passes out of the tree's leaves and back into the air.

In places where water is scarce and the land very dry, farmers irrigate the land to make it possible for crops to grow. Irrigation is an artificial way of channelling water from rivers, lakes or reservoirs, or bringing water up from underground wells using pumps or buckets.

◀ An aerial view of a stretch of the River Nile where water from the river has been used to irrigate the land, making it fertile and suitable for farming. Can you see where the strip of green land ends and the desert begins?

Irrigation can make plants grow a lot bigger and more quickly than they would do without this artificial watering. Unfortunately, though, as the irrigation water evaporates in the Sun, salt builds up in the top layers of the soil and eventually the soil can become too salty for crops to grow there.

One of a series of irrigation channels on a farm in Douz, Tunisia. This artificial watering makes it possible for crops to grow on what would otherwise be barren land.

Getting water from rivers to irrigate the land can be difficult and expensive. Can you design and make a simple machine to lift water out of a model river on to the bank? The machine must use only muscle power or the power of the river.

This pump is called an Archimedes' screw. By turning the handle at the top of the screw, water is forced up the curved grooves inside the screw and out of the top.

15

Water for livestock

The overgrazing of the natural vegetation and the resulting soil erosion has made this area of land in Tunisia desert-like.

The animals that provide us with meat, milk and eggs need large amounts of clean water to drink. A dairy cow, for example, drinks 135 litres of water a day. Often, in areas where there is low rainfall, the grass doesn't grow quickly enough for the number of animals kept on it. The overgrazed vegetation dies, and the bare soil is blown away by the wind or washed away the next time it rains.

Water is also a home for millions of animals and it supplies us with one of our most important foods – fish. When people caught fish in small amounts the fish could breed and grow faster than they were caught. Nowadays giant factory ships catch vast numbers of fish, and there is a danger that we will leave too few fish in the sea to grow and breed.

The large fishing nets often catch other sea creatures which, being of no use as human food, are needlessly killed. This method of fishing has changed the balance of life in the oceans and seas and resulted in many sea animals, and people, having less food.

In some countries people breed and farm fish in tanks, ponds and lakes, or in seawater near to the shore. The large numbers of fish produce a lot of droppings and stale food. These make tiny water plants, some of which are poisonous, grow rapidly. Diseases are also spread easily between the fish, and the chemicals used to wipe them out can poison the water, other sea creatures, and the fish we eat.

▲ Salmon fishing near Vancouver Island, Canada, using a purse seine net. The long deep net encircles a whole shoal of fish and is then gradually drawn in, herding the fish into a small bag.

▼ The fish in this salmon fish farm in Norway are kept in small areas and fed on rich foods so that they grow quickly.

Surviving where water is scarce

Plants surviving in the desert have had to adapt to the dry conditions and develop ways of storing water. A cactus, for example, stores water in its thick stem. As the cactus gradually uses up the water the stem shrivels. When the next rain comes, it will store more water.

Some desert plants have long roots to reach water deep underground. The roots of the acacia tree may go down 30 metres or more to reach water, while the mesquite bush of North America sends its roots down to a depth of 50 metres.

▼ To stop water evaporating, the leaves of most cacti have been reduced to thorny spines. These also help to prevent the cacti from being eaten.

▲ **Before**

▲ ▶ The Mojave Desert in California. After a rainfall desert plants flower, and seeds which have been scattered in the desert sand start to grow. As the desert dries out again the flowers die, but the plants drop their seeds ready for the next rain.

▲ **After**

Few animals live in the desert. Those animals that can survive get the water they need from their food. Most of them sleep during the day and only come out at night.

The people who live in desert areas are experts at surviving in these very dry conditions. The Bushmen of the Kalahari Desert, for example, survive by collecting rain, digging for underground water and squeezing water out of plant roots.

▶ Camels are probably the best-known desert animals. A camel can go for three weeks without drinking. When the camel does find water it can drink 115 litres or more in a few minutes.

This Kalahari Bushman is digging for underground water. Any water he finds is sucked up through a hollow stem into an ostrich egg container.

Making a solar still

Although it rarely rains in the desert, there is often water in the soil. People who get lost in the desert can get water by cutting open cacti or by making a solar still like this.

1 On a dry sunny day, dig a hole at least one metre across and 60 centimetres deep.

2 Put a clean jar or tin in the centre and spread a polythene sheet over the hole.

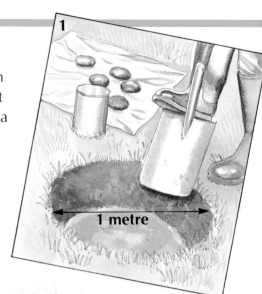

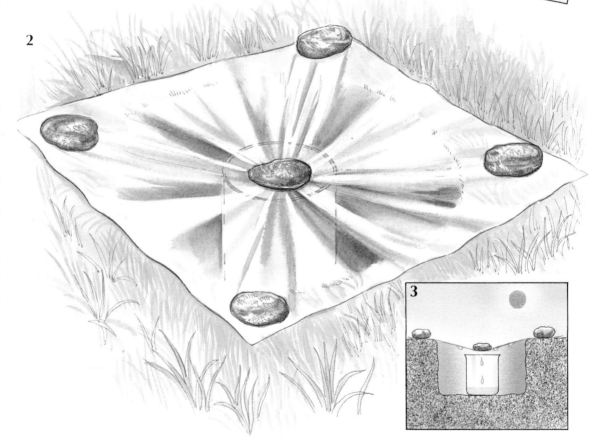

3 Fix the edges of the sheet with stones and place a flat stone in the centre of the polythene so that it sags towards the tin or jar.

The Sun will heat the soil beneath the polythene. Moisture condenses on the underside of the polythene and drips into the jar or tin. How long does it take for the jar or tin to fill with water?

Grow a cactus garden

Cacti are not difficult to grow from seeds and are best sown in the spring or summer.

1 Put a layer of gravel in the bottom of each pot and then fill the pots with seed compost.

2 Sow the seeds on the surface and lightly cover them with fine sand.

3 Enclose each pot in a polythene bag until the seedlings appear. Keep the compost moist but not wet.

When they are big enough, plant out the seedlings to make a desert scene.

Too much of a good thing

The danger of flooding is a common and widespread problem. Although floods can sometimes be useful, helping to fertilise the nearby soil, many have disastrous effects.

In the lower parts of some rivers, the river bed is gradually raised as mud and sand settle on it. Eventually, the water rises above the level of its banks, and spills out on to the surrounding countryside.

This was Katoon in Thailand, where 300 families once lived. In half an hour, much of the population was wiped out as floods and mud slides sent boulders crashing into the flimsy wooden houses. Environmentalists blame the tragedy on illegal logging which prevents the growth of trees and other plants that trap the rainfall during the monsoon.

Often floods are the result of human activities. In Nepal, for example, large areas of forest have been cleared for firewood. When it rains, the soil is no longer held in place by the tree roots, and is washed into rivers, ruining the crops in the fields and choking the rivers with mud and silt. This is believed to cause floods hundreds of miles away in the lowlands of Bangladesh and India.

Deforestation in Nepal is believed to cause floods miles away in the lowlands of Bangladesh and India.

The Volga River in the Soviet Union used to flood regularly. But a series of huge dams built across the river to make a series of reservoirs has helped to regulate the flow of water as well as producing hydroelectricity.

▲ Tidal surges can also cause the water level at the mouth of a river to rise rapidly, flooding the surrounding area. This danger exists in the Thames Valley, in England, where a large flood barrier has been built across the River Thames to prevent flooding in London.

▲ The Aswan High Dam, built across the River Nile to protect Egypt from the Nile's yearly floods.

Unfortunately dams and reservoirs are sometimes not so successful. The reservoir, Lake Nasser, which was formed when the Aswan High Dam was built across the River Nile, was intended to protect Egypt from the Nile's yearly floods and to provide water for irrigation and hydroelectric power. However, it is slowly filling up with mud and will soon be useless.

Water for leisure

For many people living in developed countries, lakes, rivers and the sea are places to 'get away from it all', or to enjoy water sports or boating. Most of the world's best-known rivers and lakes have tourist cruises as well as tourist resorts on their shores.

Most sporting and leisure activities cause some disturbance to the wildlife of these areas. River banks are worn away by the wash from boats and, in many areas, the water has become polluted with litter and oil from boats. Too many tourists in the area can also mean heavy demands on drinking water and not enough for the needs of local people.

▼ The banks of rivers and lakes in or near towns and cities are among the few places where people can enjoy a bit of peace and quiet. There is, however, a growing demand for such areas to be used for boating activities and fishing.

◄ One of the many floating hotels which cruise the River Nederrijn in Holland.

▼ The river banks of this Italian river are gradually being worn away by the wash from the many boats which use the river.

What you can do

✳ Walk quietly near lakes and rivers so that you do not disturb the wildlife.

✳ Save water (see page 11).

✳ Never leave litter.

Water pollution

Factory outflows such as this one into an Italian river are killing water plants and animals and making the water unfit for human use.

▼ After the wreck of a large tanker, this coastline has been heavily polluted by oil.

Each year, thousands of tonnes of human sewage and poisonous chemicals are pumped into our streams, rivers and seas. This dirtying or poisoning of water is called pollution.

Oceans and seas are also being polluted by oil spilled into them from ships and drilling rigs, while some factories and industries use the sea as a dumping ground. Human visitors to beaches also pollute the sea by leaving litter. The Mediterranean Sea is one of the filthiest seas in the world. It is estimated that about 430 billion tonnes of pollution enter the Mediterranean each year.

◀ This cormorant has been contaminated by oil, and the bird's wings have been further damaged by its efforts to clean them.

25

Lakes such as this one in Sweden are dying due to the high level of acid they contain. The helicopter is dumping lime into the lake in an attempt to neutralize the acid.

The fertilisers and pest killers that farmers put on fields also contribute to water pollution, as they get washed into streams, rivers and lakes when it rains.

▶ This scientist is collecting water samples from one of Sweden's dying lakes to monitor the level of acidity. She can also get an idea of how polluted the water is by looking at the kinds of small animals and plants living in it.

What happens when water becomes polluted?

1 Fill five clean jamjars with the same amount of either rain water or clean pond water.

2 Stand the jars on a sunny windowsill.

3 After a few days the water in the jars will go green. This is because tiny plants called algae grow in it. Similar algae grow in ponds, rivers, streams, lakes and the sea.

4 Into the first jar put a small amount of lubricating oil, into the second a small amount of detergent powder, into the third a small amount of washing-up liquid, and into the fourth a small amount of vinegar. Leave the fifth jar as it is. Label the jars.

5 Watch what happens over the next few days. Record your findings.

How do you think these substances get into water? What effects do you think they would have on water plants and animals?

Acid rain, caused by gases given out by power stations, factories and motor vehicle exhausts, is also spreading pollution around the world. Acid rain not only affects the land, killing plants and trees, but drains into rivers and lakes, killing the plants and animals there.

How polluted is your local stream or river?

Copy the chart below in your notebook. Watch carefully from the bank of a stream or river. Fill in as much of the chart as you can.

If there is oil floating on the surface of the water you can usually see the rainbow patterns it makes.

Signs of polluted water		Signs of clean water	
Litter present		No litter present	
Oil on the surface		No oil	
Water is cloudy		Water is clear	
Mud smells bad		Mud smells pleasant	
Bubbles coming from mud		No bubbles from mud	
Few or no water animals		Many water animals	
Little or no water weed		Plenty of water weed	

1 Carefully collect a jar of the water. Let it stand for a few minutes and then drop a small coin into the water. If the coin is hard to see, then the water is cloudy and may be polluted.

2 Use a net to collect some of the mud from the bottom. If the mud smells bad, then the water is polluted.

3 Are there lots of animals and plants living in the water, or few, or none at all? The more animals and plants you find, the less polluted the water is.

Does your river or stream show more signs of polluted water or of clean water? Be sure to wash your hands thoroughly after touching the water or mud or, better still, wear rubber gloves.

Cleaning and conserving water

The plants and animals living in lakes, rivers and the sea can clean small amounts of water naturally. However, towns and cities with large populations produce too much waste for the water to be cleaned this way. These wastes can quickly spread deadly diseases such as cholera, typhoid and polio, as well as killing wildlife, so the water is cleaned at a sewage works before it is returned to a lake, a river or the sea. Unfortunately, though, there are still many factories, towns and cities which do not clean their waste water properly before it is returned to a lake, a river or the sea.

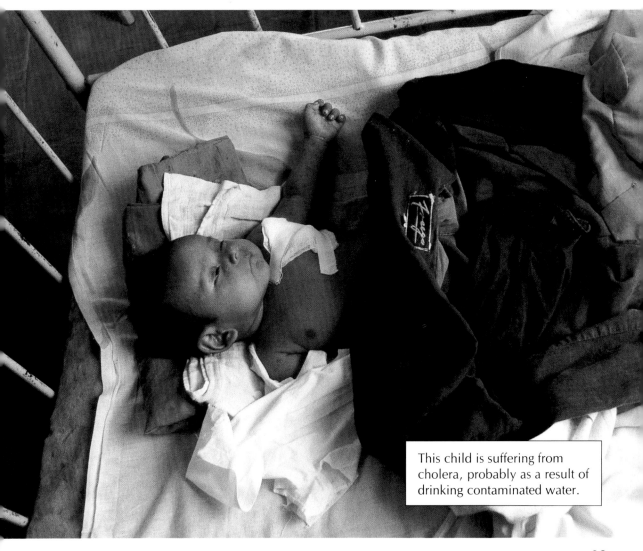

This child is suffering from cholera, probably as a result of drinking contaminated water.

In crowded parts of the world, the water which leaves one town or city will be used again fairly quickly by another further down the river. If you live in London, for example, the water has probably been drunk by six other people before you drink it! This is one very good reason why we should use water carefully and not pollute it. The water we pollute today may be the water we have to drink tomorrow.

How waste water is treated

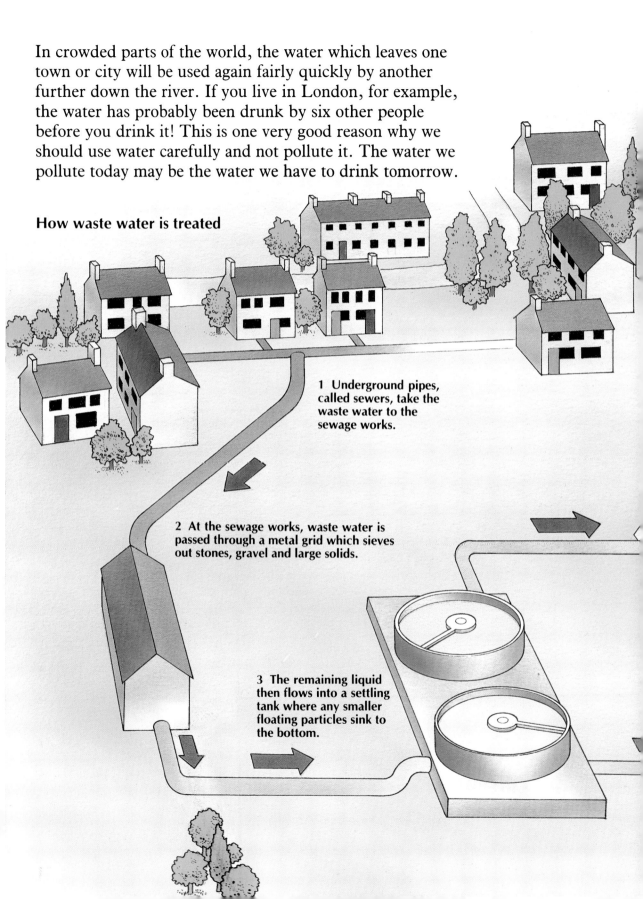

1 Underground pipes, called sewers, take the waste water to the sewage works.

2 At the sewage works, waste water is passed through a metal grid which sieves out stones, gravel and large solids.

3 The remaining liquid then flows into a settling tank where any smaller floating particles sink to the bottom.

What you can do

✳ Save electricity. Switch off heaters and lights if you are not using them. Producing electricity uses lots of water and helps to produce acid rain.

✳ If you only have a short distance to travel, walk or cycle or use public transport, rather than go by car. Poisonous car exhaust gases combine with water in the air and help to make acid rain.

✳ Don't put used oil or chemicals down the drain – they might end up polluting the sea or a river.

✳ See how little washing-up liquid you can use. Use a 'biodegradable' washing-up liquid if you can.

✳ Don't waste paper.

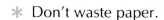

4 The sludge from the bottom of the settling tank passes into airtight tanks where special bacteria feed on it and turn it into a gas called methane. This gas can be used as a fuel to produce electricity to drive the pumps at the sewage works.

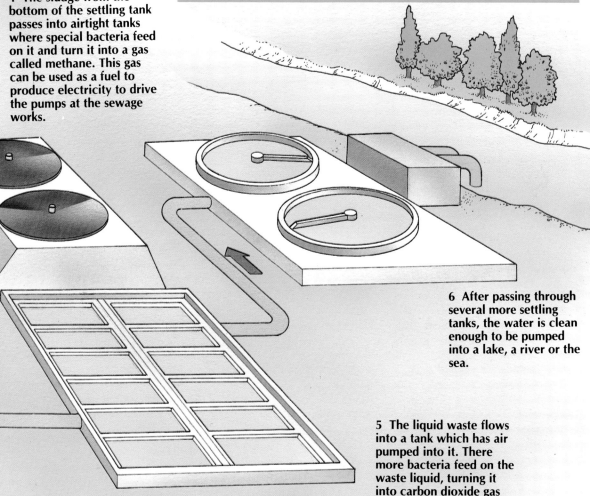

6 After passing through several more settling tanks, the water is clean enough to be pumped into a lake, a river or the sea.

5 The liquid waste flows into a tank which has air pumped into it. There more bacteria feed on the waste liquid, turning it into carbon dioxide gas and water.

31

Useful addresses

If you would like to find out more about the ideas in this book, write to any of these organisations:

Council for Environmental Education,
School of Education, University of Reading, London Road, Reading, RG1 5AG.
Friends of the Earth (UK),
26–28 Underwood Street, London, N1 7JQ.
Friends of the Earth (Australia),
Chain Reaction Co-operative, P.O. Box 530E, Melbourne, Victoria 3001.
Friends of the Earth (New Zealand),
P.O. Box 39-065, Auckland West.
Greenpeace (UK),
30–31 Islington Green, London, N1 8XE.
Greenpeace (Australia),
Studio 14, 37 Nicholson Street, Balmain, New South Wales 2041.
Greenpeace (New Zealand),
Private Bag, Wellesley Street, Auckland.
National Rivers Authority,
Rivers House, 30–34 Albert Embankment, London, SE1 7TL.
Watch,
The Green, Witham Park, Lincoln, LN5 7JR.
WaterAid,
1 Queen Anne's Gate, London, SW1H 9BT.
Water Authorities Association,
1 Queen Anne's Gate, London, SW1H 9BT.
World-Wide Fund for Nature (WWF-United Kingdom),
Panda House, Weyside Park, Godalming, Surrey, GU7 1XR.

Index